How to Stay Mentally Healthy:

A Guided Workbook

to

Self-Awareness

and

Self-Discovery

Nathalie Dorléans Ellis, LPC

Copyright and Proper Use Notice

Please note that copyright and other laws protect these materials.

Copyright 2020 by Nathalie D. Ellis, LPC, NCC

All rights reserved. Distributed under license by ESTEEM Counseling and Consulting Services, LLC. These materials are for your personal use only. This material may not be rested, leased, sublicensed, distributed, redistributed, or reproduced in any manner whatsoever, in whole or in part, without the written permission of ESTEEM Counseling and Consulting Services, LLC.

These methods and materials may not be laced on the website, server, or any other public location. This permission is reserved as the sole province of ESTEEM Counseling and Consulting Services, LLC.

Workbook Developer: Nathalie D. Ellis, LPC, NCC, CPCS

ESTEEM Counseling and Consulting Services, LLC

4290 Memorial Drive Suite B Decatur, GA 30032

info@esteemcounselingservices.com

Visit us on the web at:

www.esteemcounselingservices.com

www.facebook.com/esteemcounselingservices

www.instagram.com/esteemcounselingservices

www.twitter.com/esteemcounselingservices

www.linkedin.com/nathalieellis

Introduction

Creating this workbook, "How to Stay Mentally Healthy: A Guided Workbook to Self-Awareness and Self-Discovery", has been a long journey. It was inspired through my work with clients. Because I am a visual person, I would often find myself drawing a picture or a concept on a piece of paper to explain and show to clients. So I figured, rather than continue to make the visual over and over again and collect lots of pieces of paper, why not put it all in a book, a workbook. This guided workbook is a compilation of ideas, activities, concepts, strategies, and tools that I use with my clients as they HEAL THY SELF in therapy. I am so grateful to have completed this workbook and provide it to you all. I am an advocate of mental health wellness and my mission is to Empower, Enrich, Educate and Motivate Self and Others.

This workbook is designed to help you become self-aware which can lead to self-discovery and have a better understanding of one's mental health. I do believe that the more self-aware that we are through enrichment and education, the more empowered we can be to cope with, manage, and face our struggles, and in turn eventually heal.

Thank you for getting this workbook and let us begin the journey to staying mentally healthy through self-awareness and self-discovery.

As you begin your journey, help me spread the importance of mental health and mental wellness to others by tagging a picture with your workbook at **@esteemsguidedworkbooks** on your social media platforms. "Break the Silence, Break the Stigma, Break the Shame surrounding Mental Health".

Guided Workbook Format

Lesson- The information that I am teaching about and the purpose relating to mental health.

Activity- Self-awareness and self-discovery activity to work on regarding the lesson.

Reflective Journaling- Space to reflect and write on your awareness and discovery in relation to the lesson.

This is a workbook you can do over and over and over again (by reprinting pages) depending on where you are in your journey and healing process. This guided workbook is FOR YOU to become aware and to discover You and your mental health. **There is no wrong answer.**

Table of Contents

Common Mental Health Terminologies   6

What is the ACE Score?   8

Messages I Learned About Me   13

Messages I learned About Others/World around Me   15

My Thoughts   17

My Feelings   22

My Body Sensations   26

My Actions   28

My Thinking, Feeling, Sensing, Acting Connection   30

My Self-Portrait   34

Who Am I (Describe Me)   36

My Perfect Self vs. My True Self vs. My Hidden Self   44

My Boundaries   46

My Coping Strategies   49

Affirmations (Honoring Self)   51

Diaphragmatic Breathing and Visualization   53

Book Recommendations   55

Resources   56

About the Author   57

Thank You   58

Common Terminologies

Antidepressant-drugs used to prevent or relieve depression

Anxiety-is an emotion characterized by feelings of tension, worried thoughts and physical changes like increased blood pressure. People with anxiety disorders usually have recurring intrusive thoughts or concerns. They may avoid certain situations out of worry. They may also have physical symptoms such as sweating, trembling, dizziness or a rapid heartbeat

Bipolar-also known as manic depression, is a mental illness that brings severe high and low moods and changes in sleep, energy, thinking, and behavior

Counseling-focusing on the present events and how it affects the present

Depression-is a common and serious medical illness that negatively affects how you feel, the way you think and how you act causing feelings of sadness and/or a loss of interest in activities once enjoyed, emotional and physical problems, and can decrease a person's ability to function at work and at home

Diagnosis-the identification of the nature of an illness or other problem by examination of the symptoms

Distress-unpleasant feelings or emotions that impact your level of functioning

Healthy-things (people, thoughts, foods, actions) that are productive to your overall functioning and emotional, mental, physical health

Licensed Mental Health Professional-is a health care practitioner or social and human services provider who offers services for the purpose of improving an individual's mental health or to treat mental disorders requiring a minimum of a Master's Degree

Mental Health-The American Psychiatric Association (APA) defines mental illness as any number of health conditions that involve changes in a person's behavior, emotions, or thinking

Mental Wellness-According to the World Health Organization, mental wellness is defined as "a state of well-being in which the individual realizes his or her own abilities, can cope with the normal stresses of life, can work productively and fruitfully, and is able to make a contribution to his or her community

Mental Illness-The American Psychiatric Association (APA) defines mental illnesses as health conditions involving changes in emotion, thinking or behavior (or a combination of these), associated with distress and/or problems functioning in social, work or family activities.

Mood Stabilizers-is a psychiatric pharmaceutical drug used to treat mood disorders characterized by intense and sustained mood shifts

Psychologist-a philosophy doctor or doctor in psychology (Ph.D. or Psy.D.) who specializes in the study of mind and behavior or in the treatment of mental, emotional, and behavioral disorders: a specialist in psychology

Psychiatrist-is a medical doctor (an M.D. or D.O.) who specializes in mental health, including substance use disorders. Psychiatrists are qualified to assess both the mental and physical aspects of psychological problems

Psychotherapy (therapy for short)- mental health treatment that focuses on the past and how it affects the present

Stress-a feeling of emotional strain and pressure

Trauma-is a deeply distressing or disturbing experience causing an emotional response. Immediately after the event, shock and denial are typical. Longer term reactions include unpredictable emotions, flashbacks, strained relationships and even physical symptoms like headaches or nausea

Unhealthy-things (people, thoughts, foods, action) unproductive to your overall functioning and emotional, mental, or physical health

What is Your ACE Score?

As you begin this guided workbook, it is important to understand that who you are today is based on a number of factors, including, genetics, experiences, relationships, etc. But to begin, I want to be mindful of your childhood experiences and how they may have impacted who you are today. Let us begin.

Adverse Childhood Experiences (ACE) Study

The Adverse Childhood Experiences Study (ACE Study) is a research study conducted by the U.S. Health Maintenance Organization, Kaiser Permanente, and the Centers for Disease Control and Prevention. Participants were recruited to the study between 1995 and 1997 and have since been in long-term follow up for health outcomes. The study has demonstrated an association of adverse childhood experiences (ACEs) with health and social problems across the lifespan. The study has produced many scientific articles, conference and workshop presentations that examine ACEs.https://www.cdc.gov/violenceprevention/acestudy/about.html

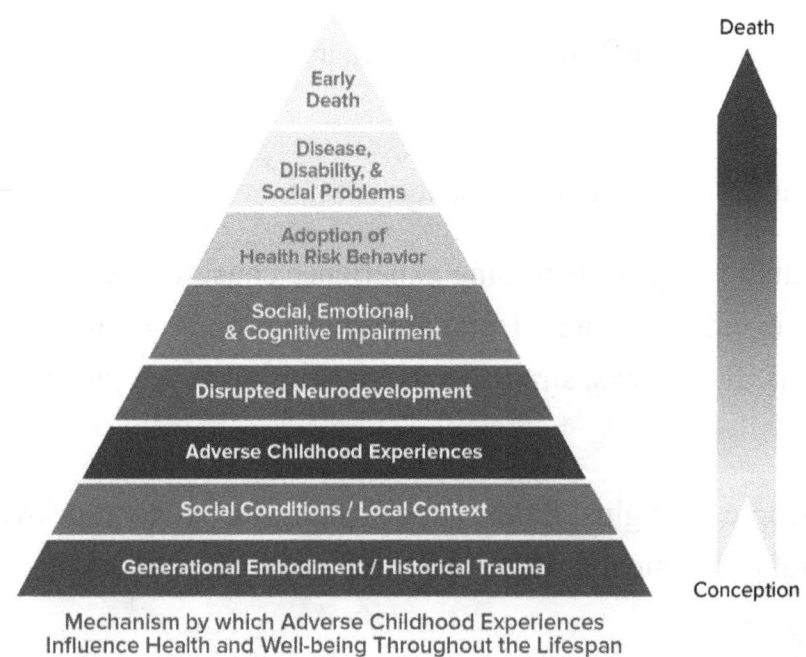

Mechanism by which Adverse Childhood Experiences Influence Health and Well-being Throughout the Lifespan

According to the Center for Disease Control, the ACE Study revealed these findings:

- Nearly two-thirds (64%) of adults have at least one adverse experience.

- High ACE scores cause adult onset of chronic disease, such as cancer and heart disease, as well as mental illness, violence and being a victim of violence
- ACEs don't occur alone….if you have one, there's an 87% chance that you have two or more.
- The more ACEs you have, the greater the risk for chronic disease, mental illness, violence and being a victim of violence.
- ACE Study shows that childhood adversity contributes to most of our major chronic health, mental health, economic health and social health issues.
- On a population level, it doesn't matter which four ACEs a person has; the harmful consequences are the same. The brain cannot distinguish one type of toxic stress from another; it's all toxic stress, with the same impact.
- Risk factors: people with an ACE score of 4 are twice as likely to be smokers and seven times more likely to be alcoholic. Having an ACE score of 4 increases the risk of emphysema or chronic bronchitis by nearly 400 percent, and attempted suicide by 1200 percent. People with high ACE scores are more likely to be violent, to have multiple marriages, more broken bones, more drug prescriptions, more depression, and more autoimmune diseases. People with an ACE score of 6 or higher are at risk of their lifespan being shortened by 20 years.*

Cultural and ethnic considerations

https://www.cdc.gov/violenceprevention/acestudy/about.html

Knowing your ACE Score is useful because it can be used for prevention and intervention, as well as, better understanding of self.

Find out your ACE Score by filling out the questionnaire on the next page. Please feel free to STOP, if you are feeling any distress when answering the questions and take deep breaths and/or contact a mental health professional.

SAMHSA's National Helpline- 1-800-662-HELP (4357)

Directions:

People have an ACE score of 0 to 10. Each type of trauma (YES) counts as one, no matter how many times it occurs. You can think of an ACE score as a cholesterol score for childhood (age 0-18) trauma.

Adverse Childhood Experience (ACE) Questionnaire

Finding your ACE Score while you were growing up, **during your first 18 years of life (circle yes or no)**:

NOTE: If you begin to feel distress, STOP and TAKE DEEP BREATHS and PACE YOURSELF

1. Did a parent or other adult in the household often ... Swear at you, insult you, put you down, or humiliate you? or Act in a way that made you afraid that you might be physically hurt?
Yes or No

2. Did a parent or other adult in the household often ... Push, grab, slap, or throw something at you? or Ever hit you so hard that you had marks or were injured? **Yes or No**

3. Did an adult or person at least 5 years older than you ever... Touch or fondle you or have you touch their body in a sexual way? or Try to or actually have oral, anal, or vaginal sex with you?
Yes or No

4. Did you often feel that ... No one in your family loved you or thought you were important or special? or Your family didn't look out for each other, feel close to each other, or support each other? **Yes or No**

5. Did you often feel that ... You didn't have enough to eat, had to wear dirty clothes, and had no one to protect you? or Your parents were too drunk or high to take care of you or take you to the doctor if you needed it? **Yes or No**

6. Were your parents ever separated or divorced? **Yes or No**

How to Stay Mentally Healthy

7. Was your mother (parent/caretaker) or stepmother (stepparent/caretaker): Often pushed, grabbed, slapped, or had something thrown at her? or Sometimes or often kicked, bitten, hit with a fist, or hit with something hard? or Ever repeatedly hit or threatened with a gun or knife?

Yes or No

8. Did you live with anyone who was a problem drinker or alcoholic or who used street drugs?

Yes or No

9. Was a household member depressed or mentally ill (without ongoing treatment) or did a household member attempt suicide? **Yes or No**

10. Did a household member go to prison? **Yes or No**

Now add up your "Yes" answers: ____ This is your ACE Score

What does your ACE score mean to you?

_____
_____
_____
_____
_____

If this questionnaire triggered any emotional, psychological, and physiological distress, it is OK to acknowledge whatever you are experiencing and it is OK to seek professional help.

SAMHSA's National Helpline- 1-800-662-HELP (4357)

Copyright 2020 by Nathalie D. Ellis, LPC   Distributed under license by ESTEEM Counseling and Consulting Services, LLC

Reflective Journaling

Heal Thy Self

Messages I Learned about Me

Oftentimes, a person takes on what others say about them or to them as truth and facts and they begin to believe these messages as their own. These messages turn into values and beliefs that they carry with them at all times. So what messages did you learn in your childhood about yourself?

My Messages Activity

What did my family and different people say about me growing up?

My Mother_____

My Father_____

My Grandparents_____

My Aunties/ Uncles_____

My Teachers_____

My Friends_____

Media_____

Other _____

What did I learn from all these people about myself?

_____

_____

_____

How to Stay Mentally Healthy

Reflective Journaling

Heal Thy Self

Messages I Learned about Others and the World Around Me

Individuals learn how to be in their family, community, society, and world by the messages they hear and see around them. Let us see what messages that you continue to carry.

Them Messages Activity

What messages (verbal/nonverbal and direct/indirect) did I learn from these different family members about others/the world around me growing up?

My Mother_____

My Father_____

My Grandparents_____

My Aunties/ Uncles_____

Media_____

Other _____

Other _____

From all these messages how do I relate to others and the world around me?

_____

_____

_____

_____

_____

_____

Reflective Journaling

Heal Thy Self

My Thoughts

A person's thoughts are made up of one's perceptions, beliefs, and values stemming from their experiences starting at an early age. Depending on the experience, they may develop positive (healthy) or negative (unhealthy) thought patterns. Let us explore your thoughts.

My Thinking Pattern Activity

What are the thoughts that come to my mind the most? Then label healthy (H) or unhealthy (U) next to your thoughts.

___

___

___

___

___

___

___

___

___

___

___

Thoughts can have a snowball effect which are made worse with unhealthy thinking patterns. The goal is to become more aware of your thoughts and your thought patterns so that you can change it before it gets worse.

Common Thinking Errors

Cognitive distortion is an exaggerated or irrational thought pattern. Circle all that applies to you and write your own example:

1. **All-or-nothing thinking (also called black-and-white, polarized, or dichotomous thinking)**: You view a situation in only two categories instead of on a continuum. Example: "If I'm not a total success, I'm a failure."

My own example:_____

2. **Catastrophizing (also called fortune telling)**: You predict the future negatively without considering other, more likely outcomes. Example: "I'll be so upset I won't be able to function at all."

My own example:_____

3. **Disqualifying or discounting the positive**: You unreasonably tell yourself that positive experiences, deeds, or qualities do not count. Example: "I did that project well, but that doesn't mean I'm competent; I just got lucky."

My own example:_____

4. **Emotional reasoning**: You think something must be true because you "feel" (actually believe) it so strongly, ignoring or discounting evidence to the contrary. Example: "I know I do a lot of things well at work, but I still feel as if I'm a failure."

My own example:_____

5. **Labeling**: You put a fixed, global label on yourself or others without considering that the evidence might more reasonably lead to a less disastrous conclusion. Examples: "I'm a loser. He's no good."

My own example:_____

6. **Magnification/minimization:** When you evaluate yourself, another person, or a situation, you unreasonably magnify the negative and/or minimize the positive. Examples: "Getting a mediocre evaluation proves how inadequate I am. Getting high marks doesn't mean I'm smart."

My own example:_____

7. **Mental filter (also called selective abstraction)**: You pay undue attention to one negative detail instead of seeing the whole picture. Example: "Because I got one low rating on my evaluation [which also contained several high ratings] it means I'm doing a lousy job."

My own example:_____

8. **Mind reading**: You believe you know what others' motivations are, or what they are thinking, failing to consider other, more likely possibilities. Example: "He's thinking that I don't know the first thing about this project."

My own example:_____

9. **Overgeneralization (also called global thinking)**: You make a sweeping negative conclusion that goes far beyond the current situation. Example: "[Because I felt uncomfortable at the meeting] I don't have what it takes to make friends."

My own example:_____

10. **Personalization**: You believe others are behaving negatively because of you, without considering more plausible explanations for their behavior. Example: "The repairman was curt to me because I did something wrong."

My own example:_____

11. **"Should" and "must" statements (also called imperatives)**: You have a precise, fixed idea of how you or others should behave and you overestimate how bad it is that these expectations are not met. Example: "It's terrible that I made a mistake. That mistake was disastrous. I should never make a mistake."

My own example:_____

12. **Tunnel vision**: You only see the negative aspects of a situation.

My own example:_____

List of cognitive distortions, definitions and examples derived from Dr. Jane Bolton, www.Dr-Jane-Bolton.com

In reviewing this list of irrational thoughts, what do you notice about yourself?_____

_____
_____
_____
_____
_____
_____
_____
_____
_____

Reflective Journaling

Heal Thy Self

How to Stay Mentally Healthy

My Feelings

Feeling or emotion is defined as an emotional state; a subjective experience of emotion (American Psychological Association). Feelings change. Feelings vary. Feeling progress or regress.

My Feeling Activity

Identify 10 or more emotions that you feel and color in each feeling with different colors.

HAPPY	SAD	DISAPPOINTED	FEAR	ANGER
JOYFUL	DEPRESSED	HESITANT	REJECTED	MAD
PROUD	ABANDONED	REMORSEFUL	INSECURE	UPSET
POWERFUL	GUILTY	JUDGEMENTAL	ANXIOUS	JEALOUS
LOVING	AWFUL	DISAPPROVAL	OVERWHELMED	WITHDRAWN
PLAYFUL	EMPTY	AWFUL	INADEQUATE	HOSTIL
RESPECTED	INFERIOR	HURT	SCARED	FRUSTRATION
PEACEFUL	VULNERABLE	REJECTED	WORRIED	BITTER
ACCEPTED	IGNORED	UNMOTIVATED	ISOLATED	PISSED
CONFIDENT	ASHAMED	LET DOWN	HOPELESS	RAGE

Copyright 2020 by Nathalie D. Ellis, LPC   Distributed under license by ESTEEM Counseling and Consulting Services, LLC

Then list out each emotion that you identified from the wheel from MOST to the LEAST. And it is possible to feel numerous emotions equally.

The #1 feeling I have _____

The #2 feeling I have _____

The #3 feeling I have _____

The #4 feeling I have _____

The #5 feeling I have _____

The #6 feeling I have _____

The #7 feeling I have _____

The #8 feeling I have _____

The #9 feeling I have _____

The #10 feeling I have _____

What do you notice? _____

_____

_____

Any patterns?_____

_____

_____

Feeling Activity

What feeling tends to be on the surface (what we mostly express or what others see)? What feelings are underneath the surface?

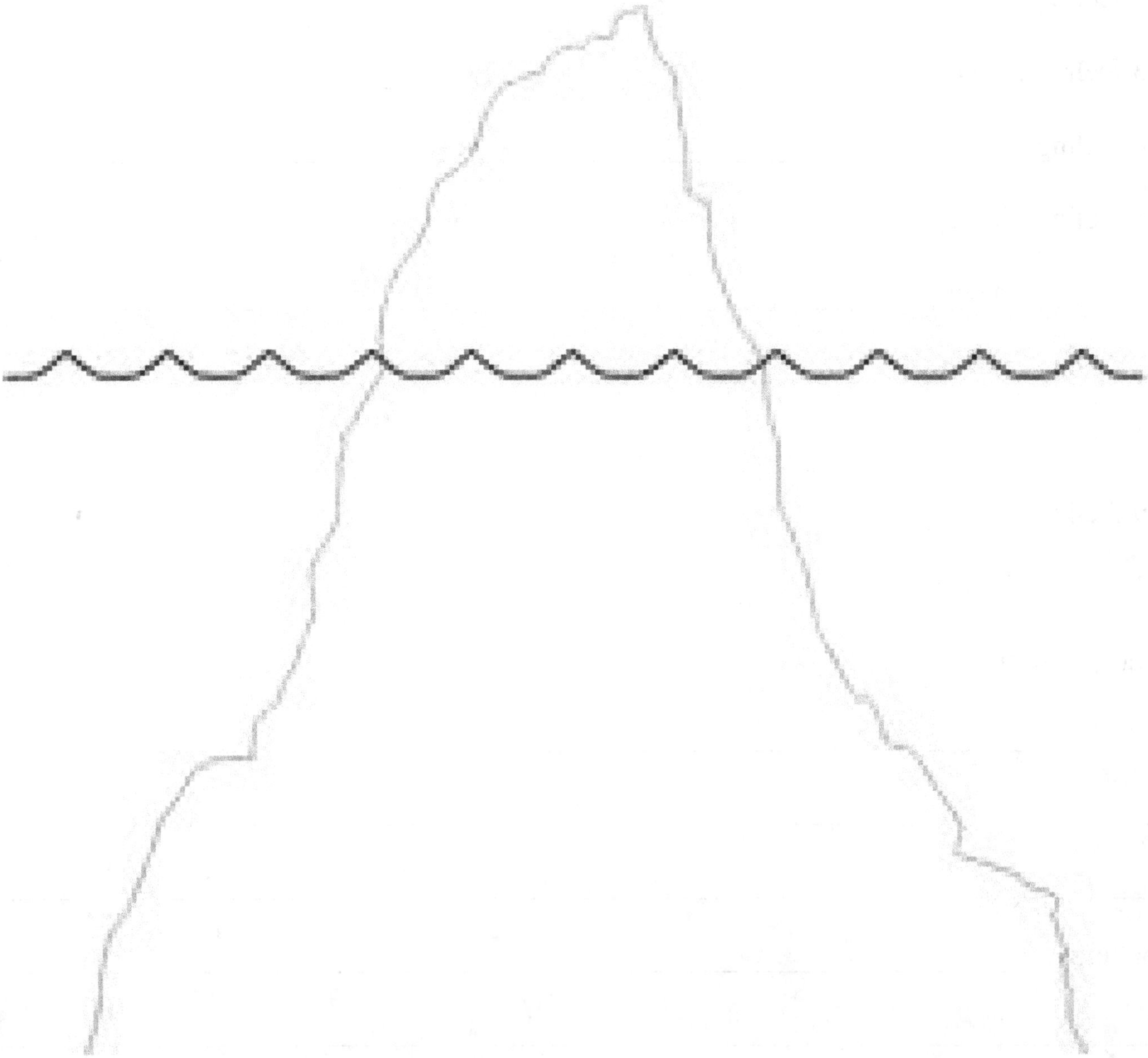

Reflective Journaling

Heal Thy Self

How to Stay Mentally Healthy

My Body Sensation

The body, too, has different feelings or sensations. It is important to notice the body because the body is connected to the mind. As shown in the ACE study, and in other research, mental health affects physical health.

Body Sensation Activity

Notice your body sensations. What do you sense on your head, face, shoulders, chest, back, arms, hands, stomach, legs, feet, etc? Write them down on the blank body.

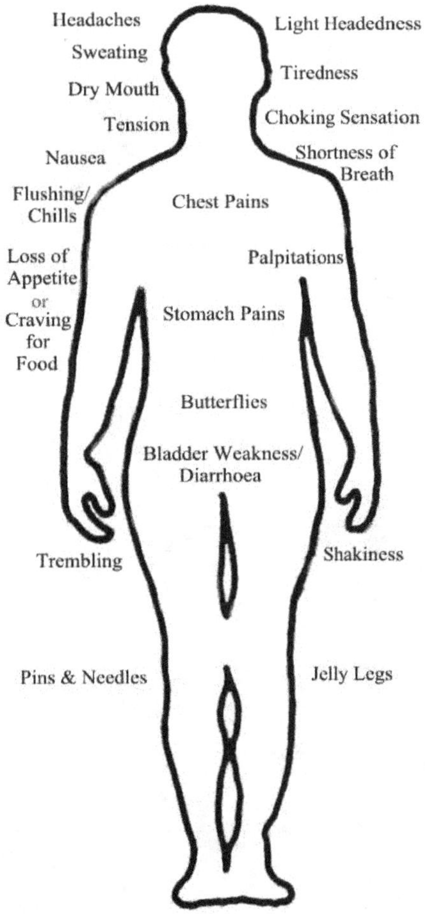

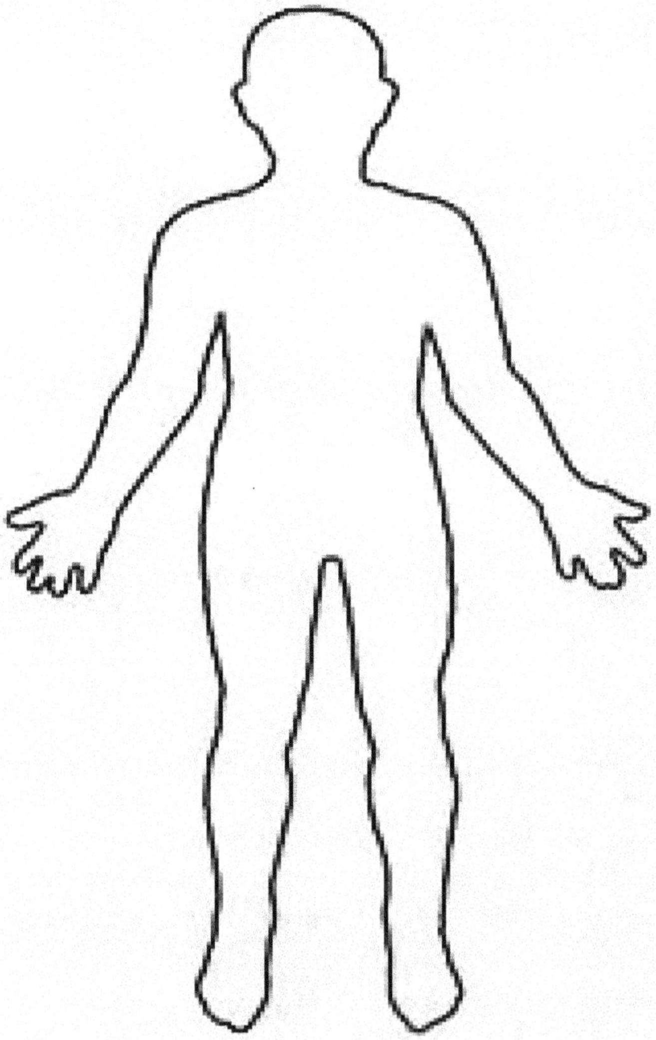

Reflective Journaling

Heal Thy Self

My Actions

Behaviors/actions are the ways a person acts and that is often a manifestation of their thoughts and feelings.

My Actions Activity

Notice your actions and write down your observations (when around certain people, when you feel a certain way, when you think certain things, when in certain situations, when in certain places).

_____
_____
_____
_____
_____
_____
_____
_____
_____
_____

Reflective Journaling

Heal Thy Self

Thinking, Feeling, Sensing, Acting Connections

How a person thinks influences how they feel, emotionally and in the body, which influences how they act and vice versa.

TFSA Connection Activity

Take one of your healthy thoughts (from the thought pattern page) and write it in the thought section. Then identify the emotion(s) that you feel as a result of that thought and write it in the emotionsection. Then identify the body sensations that you feel as a result of your emotion and/or thought and write it in the physiological section. Lastly, identify the behaviors that you felt as a result of the thought and/or feeling and write it in the behavior section.

Positive/Healthy

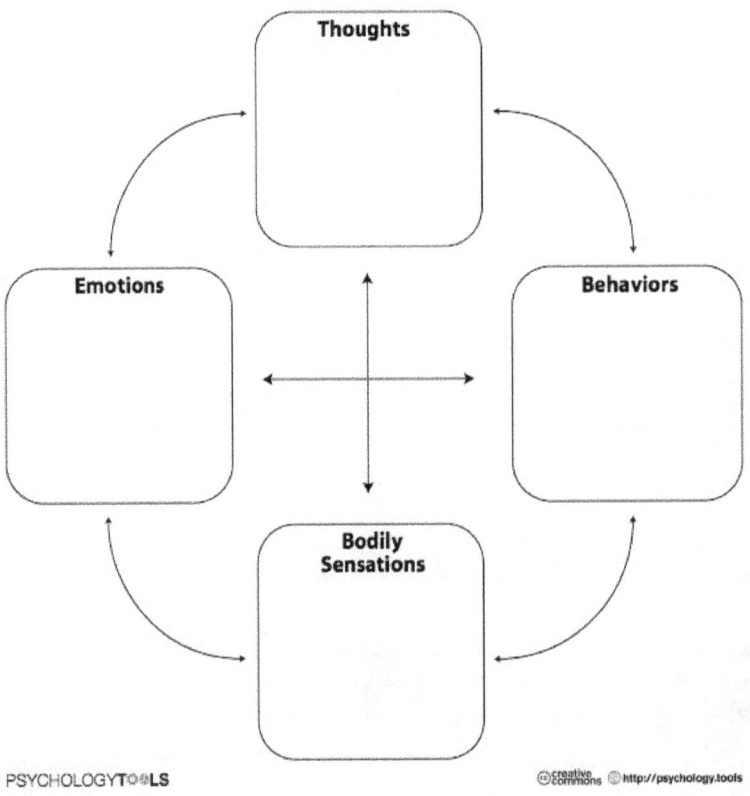

Take one of your unhealthy thoughts (from the thought pattern page) and write it in the thought section. Then identify the emotion(s) that you feel as a result of that thought and write it in the emotionsection. Then identify the body sensations that you feel as a result of your emotion and/or thought and write it in the physiological section. Lastly, identify the behaviors that you felt as a result of the thought and/or feeling and write it in the behavior section.

Negative/Unhealthy

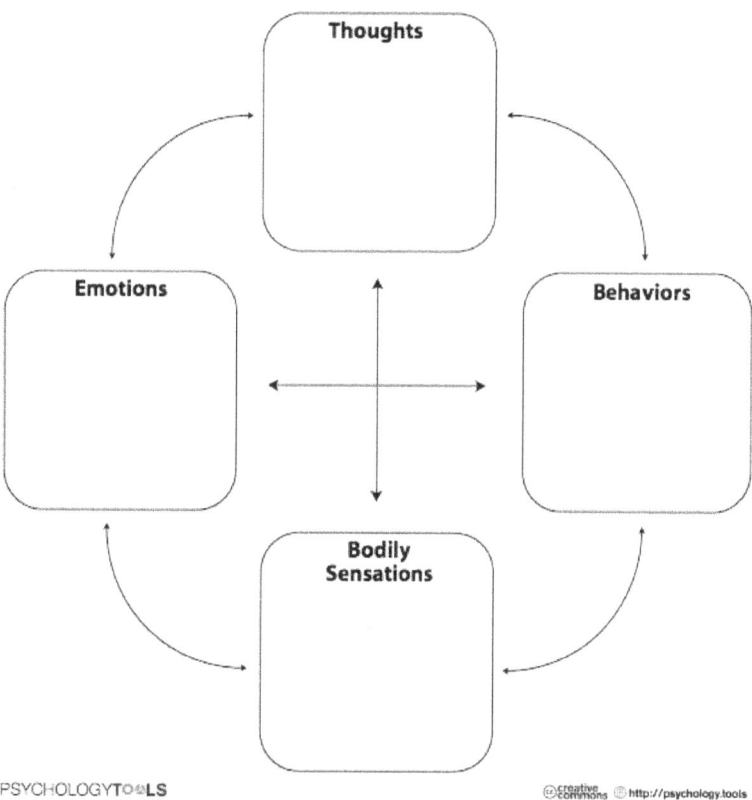

It is important to be AWARE of when you are thinking, feeling, sensing, and acting negative/unhealthy and in order to STOP the pattern and begin to be intentional in SHIFTING the mindset to a positive/healthy thinking, feeling, and acting state of mind.

AWARE ➡ *STOP* ➡ *SHIFT Activity*

A simple activity to practice shifting a negative to a positive is to simply think of the opposite. First, be aware of the negative thought, feeling, or action pattern and identify the opposite and intentionally begin a new pattern. This Activity takes a lot of practice because, initially, you are not going to believe "the positive" thought.

Example: "I am ugly" AWARE/STOP/ SHIFT "I am beautiful" ; "I can' trust anyone" AWARE/STOP/SHIFT "I can trust some people".

Practice shifting unhealthy/negative thinking to healthy/positive thoughts.

_____ ➡ _____

_____ ➡ _____

_____ ➡ _____

_____ ➡ _____

_____ ➡ _____

_____ ➡ _____

_____ ➡ _____

_____ ➡ _____

_____ ➡ _____

_____ ➡ _____

Reflective Journaling

Heal Thy Self

How to Stay Mentally Healthy

Self-Portrait

How a person sees themselves often influences how they interact with self and the others around them.

Self-Portrait Activity

Using this figure, draw a picture of YOU.

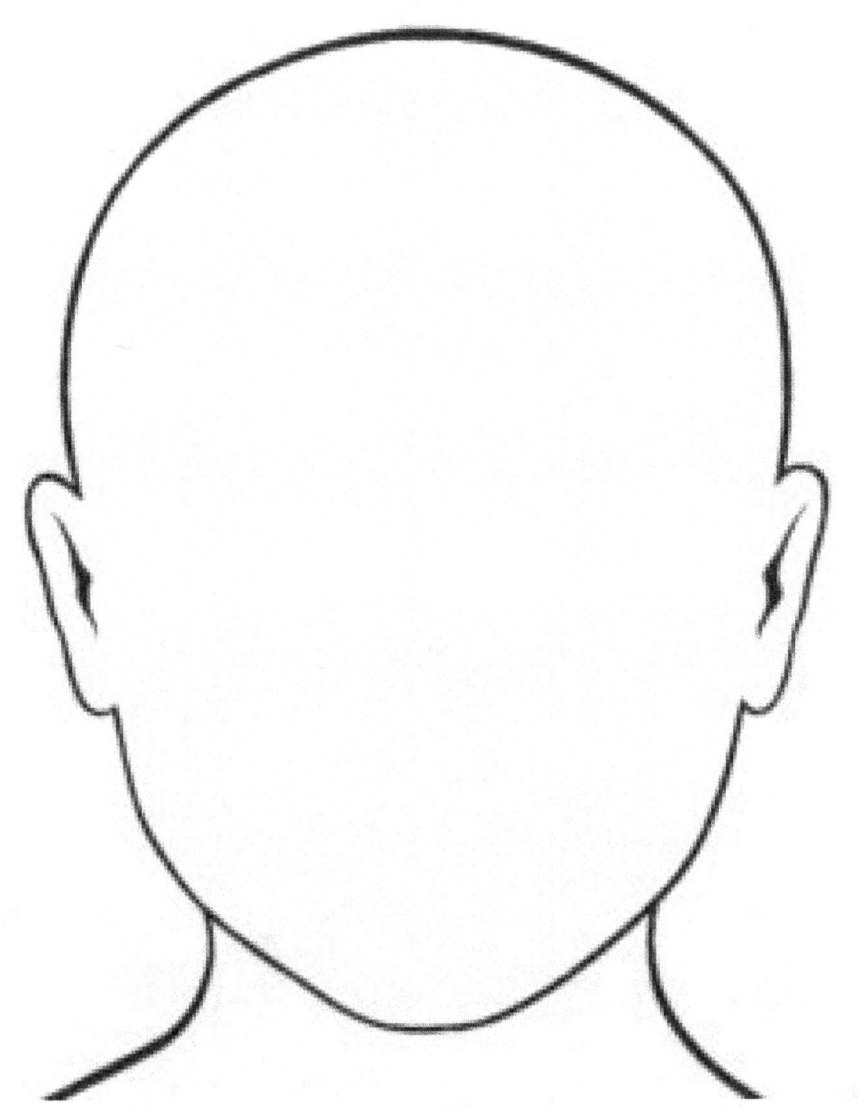

Reflective Journaling

Heal Thy Self

How to Stay Mentally Healthy

Who Am I (Describe Me)

Have you ever been asked, who are you? What do you say? find that 75% of my clients struggle with answering that question because they truly do not know who they are or if they do, they fear judgement or rejection. Who we are is fluid meaning it changes as we age, experience things, based on many things . Who we are includes the "beauty, the good, the bad, and the ugly."

Who we are consists of our personalities, values, style, physical appearance, nationality, characteristics, traits, and favorite things.

Who Am I Activities

What are My core values (Circle all that Apply):

Authenticity	Contribution	Inner
Achievement	Creativity	Harmony
Adventure	Curiosity	Justice
Authority	Determination	Kindness
Autonomy	Fairness	Knowledge
Balance	Faith	Leadership
Beauty	Fame	Learning
Boldness	Friendships	Love
Compassion	Fun	Loyalty
Challenge	Growth	Openness
Citizenship	Happiness	Optimism
Community	Honesty	Peace
Competency	Humor	Pleasure

How to Stay Mentally Healthy

Popularity	Security	Status
Recognition	Self-Respect	Trustworthiness
Religion	Service	Wealth
Reputation	Spirituality	Wisdom
Respect	Stability	
Responsibility	Success	

What are my Personality/ Character Traits (Circle all that apply):

POSITIVE	NEGATIVE
accepts what's given	ignores, rejects what's given
affectionate	distant, cold, aloof
Ambitious, motivated	unmotivated
aspiring	unsatisfied
candid	closed, guarded, secretive
caring	uncaring, unfeeling, callous
change; accepts, embraces it	rejects change
cheerful	cheerless, gloomy, sour, grumpy
considerate, thoughtful	inconsiderate, thoughtless
cooperative	uncooperative, unhelpful, combative
courageous	cowering, fearful
courteous	rude, impolite

How to Stay Mentally Healthy

decisive	indecisive
devoted	uncommitted, uncaring, hostile
determined	indecisive, unsure
does what is necessary, right	does what is convenient
perseveres, endures	relents, gives up
enthusiastic	unenthusiastic, apathetic, indifferent
expansive	kept back, tight, constricting
faith in life	life can't be trusted
faith in oneself	lack of faith in self
faith in others	others can't be relied on
flexible	inflexible, rigid, unbending, stubborn
fierce	weak
forgiving	unforgiving, resentful, spiteful
focused	unfocused, scattered
freedom given to others	authoritarian, controlling
friendly	unfriendly, distant, aloof, hostile
frugal, thrifty	Wasteful, spendthrift
generous	stingy, miserly, selfish
goodwill	ill-will, malice, hatred
grateful	ungrateful, unappreciative

hard-working	lazy
honest	dishonest, deceiving, lying
humble	arrogant, conceited, ego-centric
interested	indifferent, uncaring
involved	complacent, indifferent
jealous, not	jealous, envious, covetous
kind	unkind, uncaring, cruel, mean
mature	immature
modest	vain
open-minded, tolerant	narrow, close, small-minded, intolerant
optimistic	pessimistic
perfects	allows imperfection
persistent, sustaining	flagging, fleeting, unsustaining
practical	impractical, not viable
punctual	late, not on time
realistic	naïve, impractical
reliable	unreliable, undependable
respectful	disrespectful, rude, impolite
responsibility, takes	blames others
responsible	unreliable, undependable

How to Stay Mentally Healthy

responsive	unresponsive, unreceptive
self-confident	lack of self confidence, insecure
self-directed	directed by externals
self-disciplined	undisciplined, unrestrained, indulgent
self-esteem, high	self-esteem, confidence – low
self-giving	self-centered
self-reliant	dependent
selfless	selfish
sensitive	Insensitive, indifferent
serious	silly, trivial, petty
sincere	insincere, dishonest
social independence	social approval required
sympathetic	unsympathetic, unfeeling
systematic	unsystematic, disorganized, disorderly, random
open minded, willing to consider other opinions	closed minded, insists on own view
thoughtful towards others	thoughtless, inconsiderate, callous
trusting	suspicious, mistrusting
unpretentious	pretentious, affected, ostentatious
unselfish	selfish
willing does, willingness	stubborn, unwilling, reluctant

work comes first convenience first

List a favorite item in each category (general or specific):

Color _____

Music _____

Food _____

Dessert _____

Activity _____

Book _____

Movie _____

TV Show _____

Hobby _____

Sport _____

Flower _____

Animal _____

Season _____

Childhood Memory _____

_____

_____

What did you learn about yourself after completing all the "Who Am I" Activities?

Reflective Journaling

Heal Thy Self

How to Stay Mentally Healthy

Perfect Self versus True Self versus Hidden Self

Perfect self is the part of self you want to always present to others because it pleases, accommodates, presents well. **Hidden self** is the part of self that you keep secret from others because it consists of flaws, vulnerabilities, shame. **True self** is being honest with who you are and acknowledging all parts of self, including the good, bad, and ugly.

My 3 Self Activity

From 0 to 10 (Never to Always), what number represents each of the "Self" and write it in the center of the circle?

Perfect Self　　　　**True Self**　　　　**Hidden Self**

Identify feelings and actions associated with each "Self".

Perfect Self _____

_____

Hidden Self _____

_____

True Self _____

_____

Reflective Journaling

Heal Thy Self

How to Stay Mentally Healthy

Boundaries

Boundaries are defined as a line that marks the limit of something. Having boundaries is a way to keep a person's body, feelings, space, mind safe and protected by setting a limit. There are numerous types of boundaries, including, physical, sexual, emotional, mental, spiritual, and financial, Based on a person's experiences, they can have healthy to unhealthy boundary settings.

Protecting Your Boundary Activity

Place a heart in the most **inner** circle. That heart represents YOU. And the **inner** circle represents your Emotional, Spiritual, Physical, Mental, Sexual, etc. space. That space needs to feel and be safe, loved, stable, secure, and protected. Now, take a moment, reflect, and identify what all is in your **inner** space? Who? What?

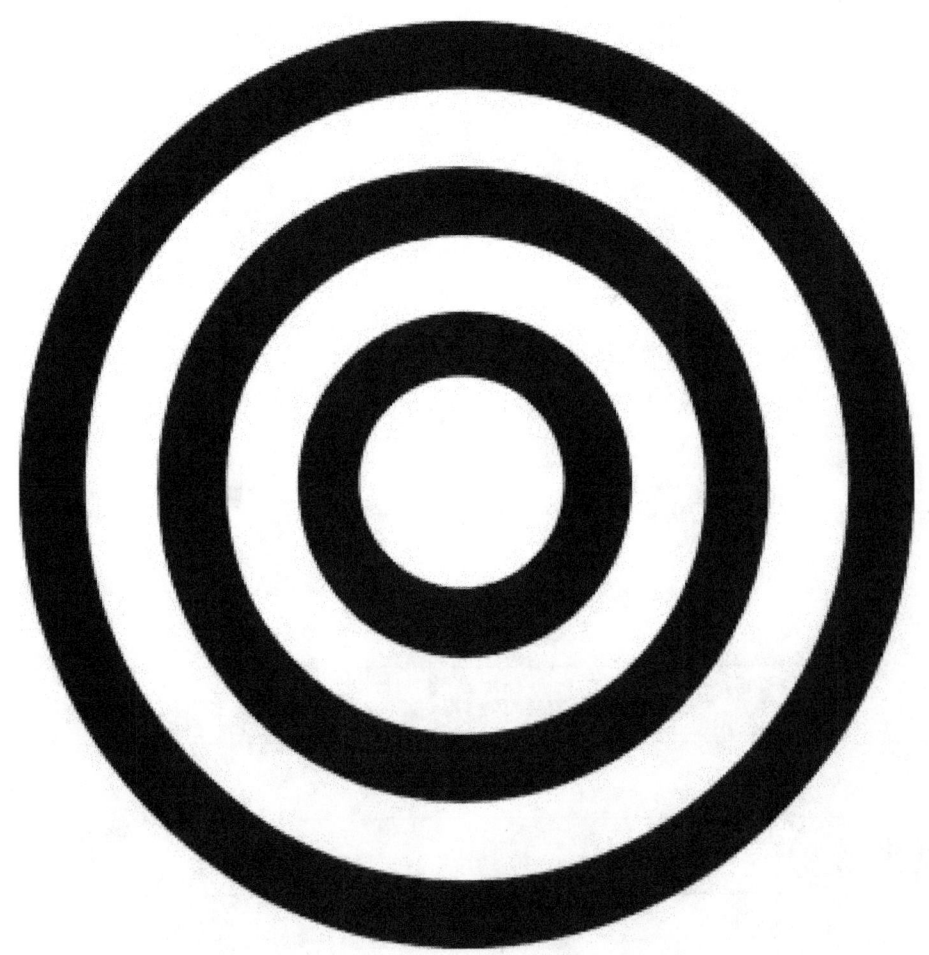

How to Stay Mentally Healthy

List out everything that you wrote in the inner circle? _____

_____
_____
_____
_____

Are the things you listed out in your inner circle protecting, building up, supporting you or destroying, tearing down, or undermining you?

_____
_____
_____
_____

Who or what in your inner circle would you move and place in the outer circles?

_____
_____
_____
_____

As you do this activity, you may notice that some of the individuals you may have to remove are your very own family member (s) and friends and that is OK.

Setting healthy boundaries is essential in maintaining your mental, physical, spiritual, health.

Reflective Journaling

Heal Thy Self

Coping Strategies

Coping is defined as a person's patterns of response to stress. So how do you cope with your stressors? There are unhealthy ways of coping and healthy ways of coping. What is your pattern of coping? Coping responses can be categorized in the following ways: ***behaviorally*** *is how you act;* ***emotionally*** *is how you feel;* ***physically*** *is how your body responds;* ***cognitively*** *is how you think.*

Unhealthy Coping Pattern Activity

Behaviorally_____

Emotionally_____

Physically_____

Cognitively_____

Healthy Coping Pattern Activity

Behaviorally_____

Emotionally_____

Physically_____

Cognitively_____

List of Immediate/ Long Term Coping Strategies to Manage Stress/Distress

Step away from the Situation   Take Deep Breaths   Tell self " I am OK"

Physical Activity   Journal   Drink Water   Go for a Walk   Exercise

Acknowledge the Stressful Situation   Express yourself   Identify your Feeling

Go on Vacation   Meditate   Pray   Set Clear Boundaries

Reflective Journaling

Heal Thy Self

Affirmations or "I Am" Statement

To affirm is to state something as a fact; assert strongly and publicly. So what facts do you want to state about yourself? In reviewing, some of your thinking, feeling, and action patterns, what have you noticed? Do you tend to affirm yourself in a positive or a negative way?

What are my Negative Affirmations?

I am _____.

I am _____.

I am _____.

I am _____.

What are my Positive Affirmations?

I am _____.

I am _____.

I am _____.

I am _____.

I am _____.

I am _____.

I am _____.

I am _____.

I am _____.

Reflective Journaling

Heal Thy Self

Diaphragmatic Breathing and Visualization

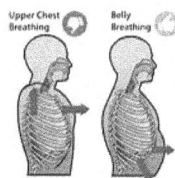

Diaphragmatic Breathing is to breathe through your nose and allow the oxygen to travel down your lungs and into your diaphragm (belly). As a result of the oxygen traveling down your belly will expand/ This proper way of breathing can calm the body and the brain when in distress.

Breathing Activity

1. Interrupt what you are doing (feeling/thinking). 2. Take a moment. 3. Be still. 4. Close your eyes or leave them open. 5. Start taking a deep breath in through your nose, let the breath travel down to your belly, and let your belly expand out, then breathe it out through your mouth. 6. Repeat step 5 ten times.

Sensory Visualization Activity

Visualization is the mental ability to restructure an image. Positive visualization mixed with sensory can calm the body and the brain when in distress.

What is a calm or happy or peaceful or safe or relaxing or fun PLACE OR ACTIVITY to you?_____

_____

1. Interrupt what you are doing (feeling/thinking). 2. Take a moment. 3. Be still. 4. Close your eyes or leave them open. 5. Visualize this place or activity. What do you see? Smell? Hear? Feel/Touch? Taste? 6. Continue visualizing for 1-2 min.

Reflective Journaling

Heal Thy Self

Book Recommendations

50 Mindful Steps to Self-Esteem: Everyday Practices for Cultivating Self-Acceptance and Self-Compassion by Janetti Marotta, PhD

It Didn't Start With You: How Inherited Family Trauma Shapes who we are and to End the Cycle by Mark Wolyn

Letting Go of Shame: Understanding How Shame Affects Your Life by Ronald T. Potter-Efron

Meditation Made Easy: More than 50 exercise for Peace, Relaxation, Mindfulness by Preston Bentley

The Body Keeps the Score: Brain, Mind, and Body and the Healing of Trauma by Besser Van Der Kolk, MD

The Body is Not an Apology: The Power of Radical Self-Love by Sonya Renee Taylor

The Developing Mind: How Relationships and the Brain Interact to Shape Who We Are by Daniel J. Siegel

The Simple Guide to Child Trauma: What It Is and How to Help by Betsy De Thierry

The Unapologetic Guide to Black MentalHealth: Navigate an Unequal System, Learn Tools for Emotional Wellness, and Get the Help You Deserve by Rheeda Walker, PhD

Resources

National Alliance for Mental Illness (NAMI)- www.nami.org

  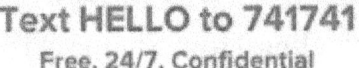 

Substance Abuse Mental Health Association (SAMHSA)-www.samsa.org

Disaster Distress Helpline Call 1-800-985-5990 or text "TalkWithUs" to 66746

National Domestic Violence Hotline – Call 800-799-SAFE (7233)

National Sexual Assault Hotline – Call 800-656-HOPE (4673)

Therapy Services

Better Help https://www.betterhelp.com/

Psychology Today http://psychologytoday.com

Talk Space https://www.talkspace.com/

Therapy for Black Girls https://therapyforblackgirls.com/

Therapy for Black Men https://therapyforblackmen.org/

APPS

Head Space https://www.headspace.com/

The Safe Place App

Not OK App https://www.notokapp.com/

About the Author

Nathalie Dorléans Ellis is Licensed Professional Counselor in the state of Georgia. She was born in Port-au-Prince, Haiti and has lived in the U.S. since age 8. She completed her Bachelor of Arts Degree in Psychology from Georgia State University in 1997. Then earned her Master of Arts Degree in Professional Counseling from Georgia School of Professional Psychology (aka Argosy University) in 2000. She has been licensed since 2001 and has worked in the field ever since. In 2012, Nathalie started her private practice and consulting agency named ESTEEM Counseling and Consulting Services, LLC where she provides therapy, training, workshop, clinical supervision, and consultation surrounding mental health. She loves physical activities (such as dancing, yoga, and walking) to relieve stress. When not working, Nathalie enjoys spending time with her son, Nathaniel, her family, and her friends.

THANK YOU

To everyone that purchased this workbook.

To my family and friends that have supported me.

To the ones who kept pushing me to stay focused and finish the workbook.

To those of you who follow and support my vision and brand.

www.ingramcontent.com/pod-product-compliance
Lightning Source LLC
Chambersburg PA
CBHW080255170426
43192CB00014BA/2676